# Christmas CRAFTS
## From around the World

Written by Judy Ann Sadler
Illustrated by June Bradford

KIDS CAN PRESS

## To Jeff, for still making every day feel like Christmas Day.

Special thanks to Mary McNeil, Mirjam Bertens Linkels, Patricia Black, Gillian Chan, Marsha Forchuk Skrypuch, Orysia Tracz, Marianne Frederiksen, Jo-Ann Horne, Vince Madamba and MaryAnn Waldrop for sharing with me their Christmas traditions. Heartfelt thanks to Maggie MacDonald, Karen Powers and June Bradford for bringing this book to life.

Text © 2003 Judy Ann Sadler
Illustrations © 2003 June Bradford

Kids Can Press acknowledges the financial support of the Ontario Arts Council, the Canada Council for the Arts and the Government of Canada, through the BPIDP, for our publishing activity.

| Published in Canada by | Published in the U.S. by |
| --- | --- |
| Kids Can Press Ltd. | Kids Can Press Ltd. |
| 29 Birch Avenue | 2250 Military Road |
| Toronto, ON  M4V 1E2 | Tonawanda, NY  14150 |

www.kidscanpress.com

Edited by Maggie MacDonald
Designed by Karen Powers
Photography by Frank Baldassarra
Printed in Hong Kong, China, by Wing King Tong Company Limited

The hardcover edition of this book is smyth sewn casebound.
The paperback edition of this book is limp sewn with a drawn-on cover.

CM 03  0 9 8 7 6 5 4 3 2 1
CM PA 03  0 9 8 7 6 5 4 3 2 1

**National Library of Canada Cataloguing in Publication Data**

Sadler, Judy Ann, 1959–
Christmas crafts from around the world / written by Judy Ann Sadler ;
illustrated by June Bradford.

(Kids can do it)
ISBN 1-55337-427-4 (bound).  ISBN 1-55337-428-2 (pbk.)

1. Christmas decorations — Juvenile literature.  2. Handicraft — Juvenile literature.
I. Bradford, June  II. Title.  III. Series.

TT900.C4S33 2003    j745.594'12    C2002-905336-6

Kids Can Press is a **ʕ⊙ᴿᴜS**™ Entertainment company

# Contents

# Introduction

*All around the world, there are hundreds of different ways to celebrate Christmas. But one thing is the same everywhere — people treasure their Christmas traditions. And for millions of people, these traditions include making crafts. They create star lanterns, golden walnuts, shiny cranberry strings, heart-shaped baskets and delicate straw ornaments. You can be part of this world celebration by making these special crafts. Surprise your family by making a British Christmas fairy; host a Mexican piñata party; count down the days until Christmas on a German Advent calendar; make Danish hearts, an Italian nativity scene, a Dutch Sinterklaas sack and more. You'll not only be making the journey to Christmas as enjoyable as the day itself, you'll be starting some wonderful new traditions.*

## MATERIALS

Many of the items you need for the projects in this book are things you may already have around home. Most of the other items are inexpensive and easy to find at fabric stores and craft and hobby shops.

### Felt

Felt is a terrific fabric. Most felt is now acrylic rather than wool or fur. It is inexpensive, does not fray and is available in many colors. You can even get felt printed with gold and silver glitter or with shiny threads running through it. It usually comes in squares or rectangles, but is also available by the meter or foot at fabric stores. Acrylic felt is not quite as soft as real felt, but it is stronger and less expensive. It is better to use real felt for the projects in this book because it is easier to glue together. However, if you can't get real felt, try gluing acrylic felt with thick white glue or ask an adult to help you use a hot-glue gun.

## Glue

Use good-quality, clear-drying, non-toxic white glue. For the star parol (page 36), use thick white glue that works well on wood. You can also use glittery or colored glue to decorate some of the projects in this book.

## Dimensional fabric paint

This paint is also known as puffy paint. It comes in a tube with a fine nozzle so that it can be used for writing words or drawing designs on fabric.

## Scissors

You will need scissors sharp enough to cut fabric and felt.

## Balsa wood

For the star parol, you will need balsa wood, which is available at hobby stores. Balsa is fragile and should be handled carefully. Buy a little extra in case it breaks. Get the thickness and width that you need and cut it into the right lengths with scissors, or score it with scissors and snap it off.

## Pipe cleaners

Pipe cleaners are also known as "chenille stems." They are available in different thicknesses, regular and sparkling tinsel colors and are usually 30 cm (12 in.) long. Cut pipe cleaners with an old pair of scissors, wire cutters or old nail clippers.

## Trim

For many projects in this book, you will need a variety of ribbon, cord, lace, buttons, beads and so on. Many fancy trims are available during the Christmas season, so choose a few special ones.

# UNITED STATES

# Cranberry and popcorn garlands

*The beauty and simplicity of strings of cranberries and popcorn, along with pretty handmade ornaments, appealed to early Americans. The tradition has continued through many generations.*
**Happy Holidays!**

1 Thread the needle with a long piece of thread.

2 Carefully poke the needle through the ends of a cranberry. If you have difficulty threading it, place the eye end of the needle on a nonslippery surface and push down gently on the cranberry. (Watch out for the point of the needle!) Slide the cranberry down to the end of the thread, knotting it there as an anchor to keep the cranberries and popcorn from sliding off the thread.

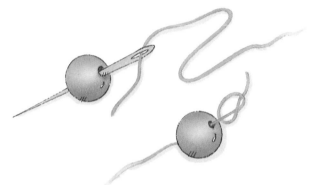

3 Thread a piece of popcorn, and slide it down the thread. Make a pattern of popcorn and cranberries, or just thread them on in no particular order. If you find the popcorn breaks easily, try a narrower needle, or allow the popcorn to sit out overnight so it gets stale and is easier to work with.

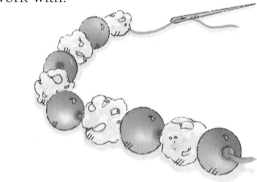

**4** When you get near the end of your thread, knot a cranberry there. Cut the thread, leaving a tail so that you can tie together many strings to make a very long garland.

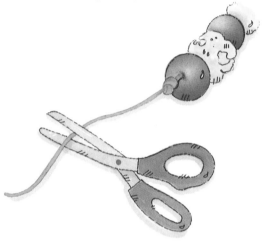

## MORE IDEAS

⭐ After Christmas, hang the cranberry and popcorn garlands outside for the birds.

⭐ Make a garland out of just cranberries.

⭐ Make a mini cranberry wreath by stringing eight to ten cranberries and knotting the thread ends together to make a circle. Add a bow and hang the mini wreath on the tree.

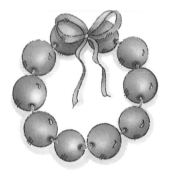

# *Felt ornaments*

Draw a simple shape, such as a heart, star, ball, bell, snowman, pear, tree or mitten, on a piece of heavy paper. Cut it out and trace it twice onto felt. Cut out both shapes. Cut a 25 cm (10 in.) piece of yarn or embroidery floss. Fold it in half and place the cut ends between the two felt shapes as you glue them together. Decorate the ornaments with glitter, dimensional fabric paint, buttons, yarn, ribbon, sequins, fancy trims or smaller felt cutouts.

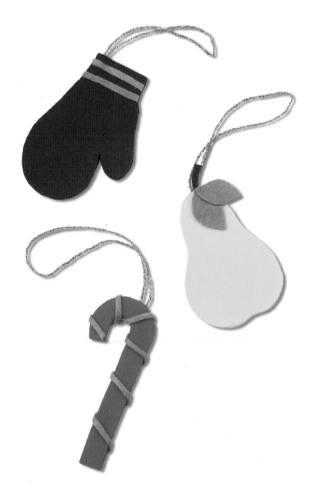

# UKRAINE
# Silver webs

*There are many charming Ukrainian folktales about spiders at Christmas. One story tells of a poor family's delight when a spider decorates their tree with silvery webs.*
**Veselykh Sviat!**

## YOU WILL NEED

- 4 silver tinsel pipe cleaners
- white or light-colored yarn (the best is one with a silver thread running through it)
- a small bead with a large hole
- a ruler, scissors

1 Cut each pipe cleaner into two pieces — one 20 cm (8 in.) and the other 10 cm (4 in.). Set aside the short pieces.

2 Twist the four longer pipe-cleaner pieces together in the center. Spread the eight ends apart evenly.

3 Wrap the yarn around the center area of the pipe cleaners a couple of times so that the yarn end will not come loose.

4 Begin winding the yarn behind, then around, each pipe cleaner about 2.5 cm (1 in.) from the center. The yarn will stick to the pipe cleaners and stay in place. When you get back to where you just started, wind the yarn a little farther out from the center.

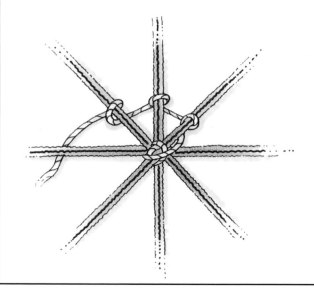

**5** Keep winding. Don't pull the yarn too tight, or the web won't stay flat. When you get to the ends of the pipe cleaners, cut the yarn leaving a 30 cm (12 in.) tail. Knot the yarn tail around one of the pipe cleaner ends and tie it into a loop so you can hang up the web.

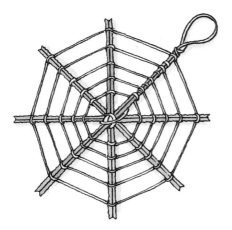

**6** To make the spider, twist the short pipe-cleaner pieces together in the center. (Or use four 10 cm [4 in.] pieces of different-colored pipe cleaners.) These will be the legs. Thread them through your bead, spread the legs and bend them downward. Place the spider on its web.

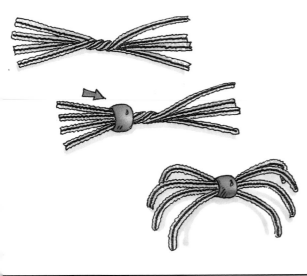

# Golden walnuts

It is also a tradition in Ukraine to paint walnuts gold and hang them on the tree. For a walnut ornament, you will need a 25 cm (10 in.) piece of yarn or gold cord or ribbon, a walnut, a nutcracker, gold acrylic craft paint, a paintbrush, white craft glue and a bead (optional).

**Note:** *If you break open many walnuts at a time, keep the halves paired together in separate cups in an egg carton, or you may have trouble matching them up again.*

**1.** Knot the ends of the yarn together to make a loop.

**2.** Crack a walnut in half. (If you have trouble breaking a walnut open evenly, try pushing a butter knife into the top and twisting it. If the walnut still breaks unevenly, that's okay. When it is time to glue it back together, apply glue along the uneven edges.)

**3.** Paint each half of the walnut and let it dry. Apply a second coat if needed.

**4.** Apply glue to the edges of the walnut halves. Place the loop knot inside and put the walnut back together. Wipe away any extra glue. Hold the halves together with a rubber band until the glue is dry.

**5.** If you like, thread a bead or two onto the cord.

# POLAND
# First star

*In Poland, it is a tradition to watch for the first star, **gwiazda**, of Christmas Eve. Carolers walk from house to house carrying a lovely gold star on a stick.*
**Wesolych Swiat!**

## YOU WILL NEED

- newspaper
- gold acrylic craft paint, a paintbrush and a container of water
- a 120 cm (48 in.) length of dowel 0.5 cm (¼ in.) in diameter
- corrugated cardboard • white craft glue
- heavy books • 2 m (6½ ft.) ribbon
- sequins, glitter, rickrack or other trimming (optional)
- a pencil, scissors, a ruler or measuring tape

**1** Spread newspaper on your work surface. Paint the dowel. Carefully place it across your container of water to dry. Add another coat if needed.

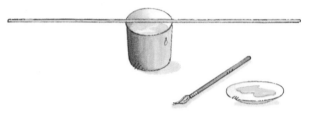

**2** Draw a large star on the cardboard. Cut out the star. Trace it onto more cardboard and cut out the second star.

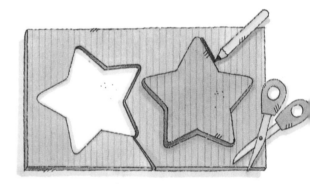

**3** Glue the stars together with the dowel glued between the two layers. Place the books on the star while the glue dries.

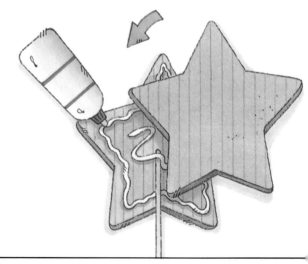

**4** Paint one side of the star. Let it dry, then paint the other side.

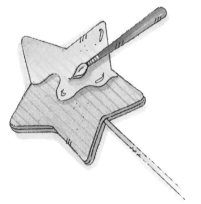

**5** Glue the end of the ribbon on the pole just below the star. Wind the ribbon down the length of the pole. Trim off the ribbon and glue the end to the bottom of the pole.

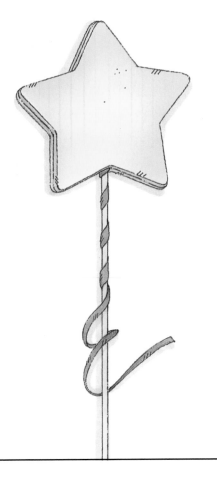

**6** Tie a bow on the stick just below the star.

**7** If you like, glue on sequins, glitter or other trim to give your star extra sparkle.

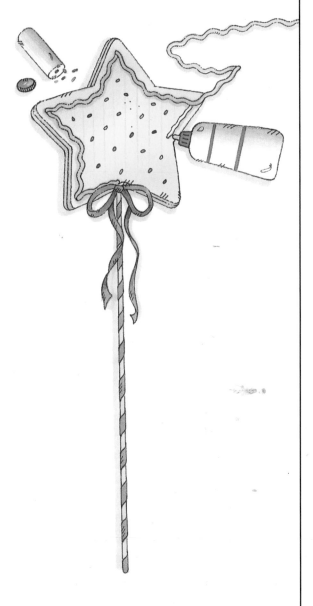

When you aren't using the star for caroling, place it in an umbrella stand, large potted plant or anywhere else that needs a festive touch.

# HOLLAND
# Sinterklaas sack

*In Holland, Sinterklaas places a burlap sack of gifts at the front door, rings the bell and dashes off to his next stop.*
### Zalig Kerstfeest!

## YOU WILL NEED

- newspaper
- 1 m (3 ft.) square of burlap (available at garden centers and fabric stores)
- supplies for decorating the sack (see step 2)
- straight pins
- a sturdy needle and thread
- cord, twine or ribbon
- a ruler or measuring tape, scissors

1 Spread newspaper on your work surface. There should be at least one side on the burlap with a selvage edge (an edge that does not fray). It is best to have a selvage edge at the top of your finished bag, so before you print the burlap, make sure this edge is the one farthest away from you.

2 Decorate the burlap in one of the following ways:

- Ask an adult to cut a potato in half and cut a star, heart, holly or other festive shape into one of the halves. Pour some acrylic craft paint or fabric paint into a pie plate or plastic foam tray. Dip the shape into the paint, then press it onto the newspaper to test it. When you are pleased with your design, print the burlap. (If you wish to change colors, rinse off the potato first.) Let it dry.

- Use dimensional fabric paint to draw a design on the burlap.

- Cut out colorful felt shapes and glue them onto the burlap.

- Use a pencil to draw a design on the burlap, then stitch the design with yarn.

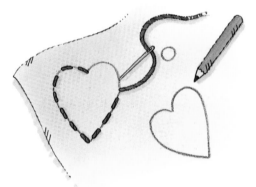

3 When you are finished decorating the burlap, fold it in half from left to right so that the designs are on the inside and the selvage edge is still at the top. Pin the edges together along the side and bottom of the sack.

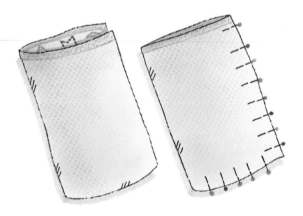

4 Thread two arm lengths of thread into your needle, double it and make a knot in the end of the thread. Sew the side and bottom of the sack with an overcast stitch, as shown, about 1 cm (½ in.) from the edge. The overcast stitch will prevent the edges from fraying. When you run out of thread or finish the seam, make a couple of stitches on the same spot, knot the thread and trim it.

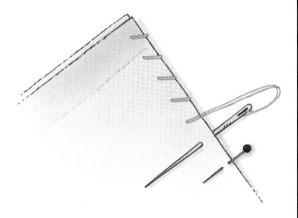

5 Turn the sack right side out. Fill it with gifts or Christmas treasures and tie it closed with the cord. For an added festive touch, fasten a couple of jingle bells onto the closure.

6 After Christmas, use the sack to store your decorations.

# CANADA
# Tree skirt

*In many Canadian homes, you'll find a freshly cut tree with a lovely skirt to cover the stand.*
**Merry Christmas!**

---

### YOU WILL NEED

- a piece of red or green felt at least 1 m (3 ft.) square
- 1 m (3 ft.) of ribbon
- assorted scraps of felt
- white craft glue
- other supplies for decorating (see step 7)
- a ruler or measuring tape, scissors

---

1 Place the square of felt on a table or the floor in front of you. Fold it in half by folding the top half down, toward you. Now fold the left side over to the right side to create a smaller square. Keep the felt in this position.

2 Cut off just the tip of the top left corner.

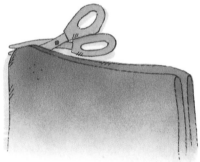

3 To make the skirt into a circular shape, round off all four layers of the bottom right corner by cutting one layer at a time.

4 Open the felt. Cut a slit from the outer edge of the felt to the center hole. Trim the center hole so that it is a smooth circle about the diameter of a Christmas tree trunk.

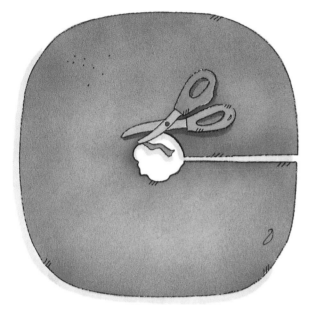

6 Snip a very small hole on each side of the slit near the center hole. Cut the ribbon in half and knot a piece into each of the two holes.

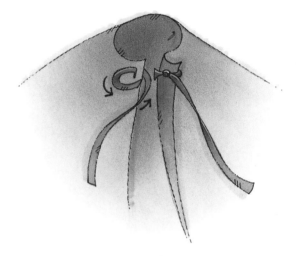

7 Time to decorate! Cut out many felt designs in the shape of polka dots and snowflakes and glue or stitch them onto the skirt. You could also use dimensional fabric paint, beads, sequins, pom-poms, glitter glue, ribbons and other decorative trims to make your tree skirt look very festive.

5 Trim all around the outer edge of the tree skirt until it is round. The edge can be smooth or scalloped.

# DENMARK
# Woven hearts

*There are hearts everywhere in Denmark at Christmas. Make these lovely woven-heart baskets, called* **hjerter**, *fill them with treats and hang them on your tree.*
### *Glædelig Jul!*

## YOU WILL NEED

- a piece of heavy paper such as bristol board or an old folder
- double-sided craft paper or shiny Christmas wrapping paper
- a ruler, a pencil, scissors

1 To make a pattern, cut a 6 cm x 20 cm (2 ¼ in. x 8 in.) rectangle of heavy paper.

2 Fold the rectangle in half. At the open end, round off the four corners.

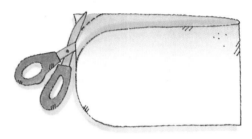

3 Unfold the pattern and trace it twice onto the wrapping paper. Cut out the two halves of your basket. Fold one in half so one color shows and fold the other in half so the opposite color shows.

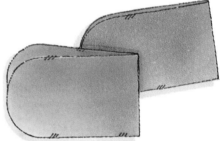

4 Tuck the one half inside the other half. Beginning at the center, make three evenly spaced 7 cm (2 ¾ in.) cuts up from the folded edge.

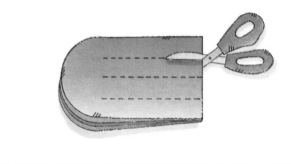

**5** Start weaving one half into the other, as shown. Tuck 1 between the layers of D, tuck C between the layers of 1, 1 between the layers of B, and A between the layers of 1.

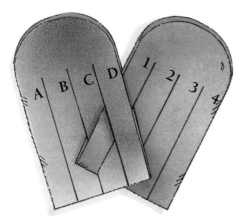

**6** Slide the woven part up a little, then tuck D between the layers of 2, 2 between C, B between 2, and 2 between A. Continue weaving until all eight strips are woven together. When you open the basket, the pattern should be on the inside as well as on the front and back.

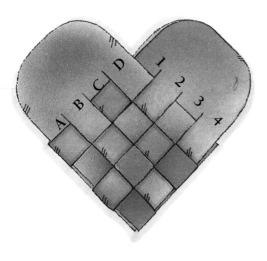

**7** Glue a handle between the two woven layers on each side of the heart.

## MORE IDEAS

★ Use your pattern to make many more woven hearts. Instead of making three even cuts, make four so that you have a wide strip, a narrow one, another wide, another narrow and yet another wide strip. This makes a neat pattern!

★ Instead of making the cuts straight, make them wavy, or use scissors with a zigzag edge.

★ Make woven hearts out of two colors of felt instead of paper. Cut tiny slits in the top and tie on narrow ribbon handles.

# MEXICO

# Party piñata

*In Mexico, the nine days before Christmas are called* **Las Posadas***. People dress up and act out Mary and Joseph's search for a place to stay. Afterwards, there are parties with music, fireworks, food and the breaking of a piñata.*
**Feliz Navidad!**

## YOU WILL NEED

- newspaper
- 1 medium-sized round or oval balloon
- 2 mixing bowls, 1 small and 1 medium
- measuring cups and spoons
- 175 mL (¾ c.) flour
- 30 mL (2 tbsp.) salt
- 350 mL (1½ c.) water
- yarn or string
- tissue paper in different colors
- small treats (see step 12 for ideas)
- white craft glue
- a blindfold, handkerchief or scarf
- a stick
- a ruler, a pencil, scissors

1 Spread newspaper on your table. Using your ruler as a guide, tear other sheets of newspaper into 4 cm (1½ in.) x 20 cm (8 in.) strips.

2 Blow up the balloon and knot it. Sit it on the small mixing bowl.

3 For papier-mâché paste, mix together the flour, salt and water in the other bowl. Use your fingers to get the lumps out.

4 Dip a newspaper strip into the paste. As you take it out, run it between your fingers to remove the extra paste. Smooth the strip onto the balloon.

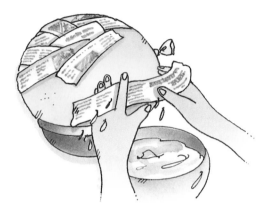

5 Criss-cross strips of newspaper all over the balloon except for an area about 8 cm (3 in.) around the knot. Turn the balloon on the bowl as you work.

6 If your papier-mâché balloon gets too wet, smooth on some dry strips. You should have four or five layers of newspaper on the balloon.

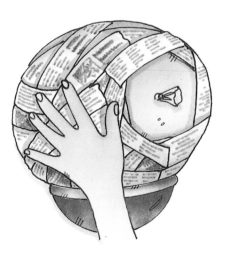

7 Leave the piñata on the bowl and turn it every few hours, or place it on a cooling rack in a warm place to dry. Depending on how wet your piñata is, it will take from one to three days to dry.

8 When you are sure the piñata is dry (check by feeling around the open edges on top), pop and remove the balloon.

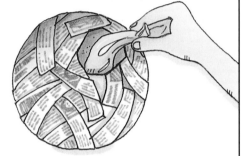

9 Use scissors to carefully poke three evenly spaced holes 2.5 cm (1 in.) down from the opening. Cut three 1 m (3 ft.) pieces of yarn or string. Pull one piece halfway through each hole and knot all six ends together.

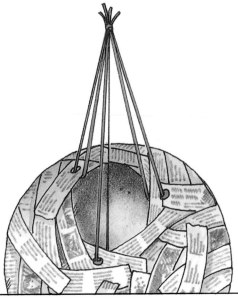

*Instructions continue on the next page* ☞

**10** Cut many pieces of colorful tissue paper into 8 cm x 8 cm (3 in. x 3 in.) squares. Poke the eraser end of your pencil into the center of a square of tissue paper, scrunch the tissue around the pencil and dip it into glue.

**11** Cover the piñata with the tissue-paper tufts. You may find this easier to do if the piñata is hanging up.When you are finished, glue many long, colorful strips of tissue paper to the bottom of the piñata for extra decoration.

**12** Fill the piñata with wrapped candies, nuts, coins, jokes and other surprises. Be careful not to make it too heavy. Hang it from the ceiling or a tree, or tie it on a broomstick and have someone hold it up high. Now you are ready for a piñata party.

Everyone should stand in a circle around the piñata. One player at a time is blindfolded, turned around three times and given a stick. Each player has three chances to try to whack the piñata. Everyone takes turns until someone breaks the piñata and the goodies spill out. All the players get to share the treats!

# SOUTH AFRICA
# Crinkle-paper chain

*In South Africa, children make these colorful box chains out of crinkle paper, or crêpe paper, to welcome Christmas into their homes. They are perfect for decorating doorways, windows, walls and trees.*
**Merry Christmas!**

### YOU WILL NEED

- 2 or more different-colored sheets of crêpe paper
- a pencil (optional) • a glue stick
- a ruler, scissors

**1** Crêpe paper is stretchy one way and has fine lines on it. Cut the crêpe paper into strips about 2.5 cm (1 in.) wide along the stretchy side, so the fine lines go across the strips. To make the cutting easier, leave the crêpe paper folded and cut through many layers at a time. The strips do not need to be perfectly straight or all exactly the same width, but if you like you can use a ruler and pencil to mark the strips before you cut them. Cut a few strips from each color of crêpe paper.

**2** Glue the ends of two different-colored strips to form a corner.

**3** Fold one strip, then the other, across the corner. You will be folding one strip up and down and the other left and right.

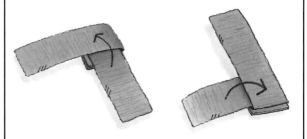

**4** Keep folding the strips together, trying to keep the folded stack square, until you run out of one or both colors. Glue a new strip to the tail end of the old one. The new strip can be a different color.

**5** Make your chain as long and colorful as you'd like. When you are finished, glue the ends together to hold the folds.

# AUSTRALIA

# Festive pillowcase

*On Christmas Eve, children in Australia and New Zealand place a pillowcase at the foot of the bed with the hope that it will be filled with small gifts and candy.*
**Merry Christmas!**

## YOU WILL NEED

- a 115 cm (45 in.) x 85 cm (33 in.) piece of cotton Christmas-print fabric
- straight pins • a needle and thread
- an iron
- scissors, a ruler or measuring tape

**1** Fold the fabric, right sides together, so that the selvage edges (the edges that don't fray) match. Pin the fabric together at the side and one end of the pillowcase.

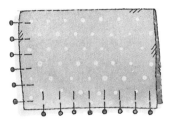

**2** If you have a sewing machine, ask an adult to help you use it. Otherwise, you can stitch the pillowcase by hand. Thread an arm length of thread into the needle. Make a knot at the end of the longer part of the thread.

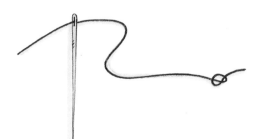

**3** Backstitch the pinned areas of the pillowcase, as shown. The stitches should be small and even, about 1.5 cm (⅝ in.) from the edge of the fabric.

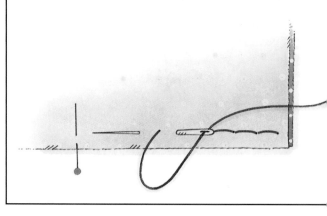

**4** When you run out of thread, make a few stitches on the same spot and cut the thread. Thread another arm length of thread into the needle, knot it and keep sewing. When you are finished, make a few stitches on the same spot to fasten the thread, then trim it. Remove the pins.

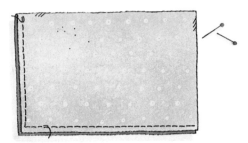

**5** Use an overcast stitch, as shown, across the end seam to prevent the fabric from fraying.

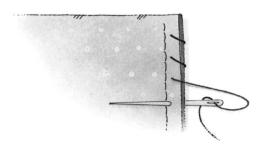

**6** Ask an adult to help you fold over and iron 1 cm (½ in.) of the fabric at the open end of the pillowcase. The wrong sides should be together.

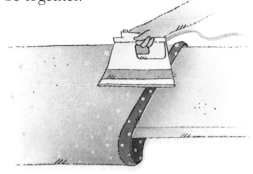

**7** Fold over and press 2.5 cm (1 in.) along the same edge. Pin it.

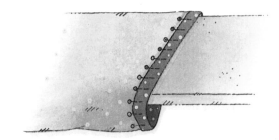

**8** Backstitch around the opening. Make sure you are stitching far enough away from the edge to be stitching through three layers of fabric. Remove the pins as you sew.

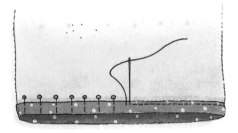

**9** Turn the pillowcase right side out and ask an adult to help you press it.

This pillowcase is perfect for sleeping on, giving as a gift, using to wrap a gift (tie it closed with ribbon) or for placing at the foot of your bed on Christmas Eve!

# BRITAIN
# Christmas fairy

*In Britain, children place a lovely fairy on or near the top of the tree. Why not start this tradition in your home?*
**Happy Christmas!**

**1** To make the fairy's dress, cut a 25 cm (10 in.) x 15 cm (6 in.) rectangle of felt. If you are using lace, cut a piece the same size.

**2** If you have lace, place it over the felt. Thread one-and-a-half arm lengths of thread into the needle. Double the thread and knot it at the end. Make a running stitch, as shown, 0.5 cm (¼ in.) from one long edge of the felt.

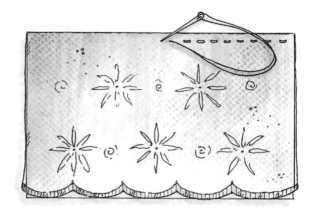

**3** When you reach the end, pull the thread tight to gather the felt. Make a couple of stitches on the same spot to hold the gathers together. Don't cut the thread.

**4** To finish the dress, pin then stitch the felt together down the back. Make a couple of stitches in the same spot and cut the thread.

**5** Bend a white pipe cleaner in half. Thread the button onto one end of the pipe cleaner and slide it to the center. Poke both pipe-cleaner ends into the bead and slide it up to the button hat.

**6** Slide the ends of the pipe cleaner into the center of the dress. Squirt glue around the neck of the dress, then pull the pipe cleaner from below so the head touches the glue.

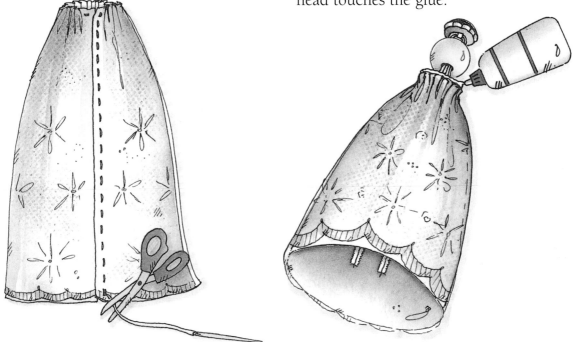

*Instructions continue on the next page* ☞

**7** Tightly wrap the second white pipe cleaner just below the neck area of the dress. Twist it twice at the back and bring the ends forward to make arms. Trim off the pipe-cleaner ends so they are the right length for arms. Slide on small beads for hands.

**8** To give your fairy a waist, tightly knot a piece of doubled yarn around her middle.

**9** For hair, cut four to six 20 cm (8 in.) pieces of yarn. Tie them under the button hat. Braid the hair, knot it into a bun or let it hang down.

**10** For wings, cut a 60 cm (24 in.) x 20 cm (8 in.) piece of tulle. Fold it until it is 15 cm (6 in.) x 10 cm (4 in.). Gather the center area by fastening it with the third white pipe cleaner. Use the pipe-cleaner ends to fasten the wings to the fairy's back. Cut off the leftover pipe-cleaner pieces.

**11** Draw (or paint) a face on your fairy.

**12** For a magic wand, make 9 tiny bends in the center area of the tinsel pipe cleaner. Twist the pipe cleaner together below the bends and shape a star. Twist the rest of the pipe cleaner together and trim the wand to the size you want. Fasten it in your fairy's hand.

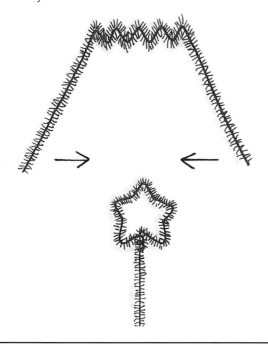

**13** Shape a tiny silver tiara out of a small piece of leftover tinsel pipe cleaner and tuck it into her hair.

**14** It is optional to cut a lace, tulle or netting shawl and wrap it around your fairy. Place your Christmas fairy on the top of your tree, on a table or shelf, or attach a sparkling string and let her fly!

# FINLAND
## Straw ornaments

*In Finland, straw ornaments play an important part in decorating for Christmas.*
**Hyvää Joulua!**

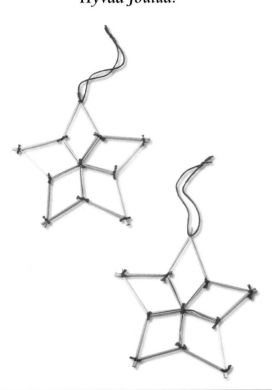

**1** Cut the head and woody ends off the wheat, and remove any loose bits along the stems.

**2** Place the stem pieces in a small amount of water in the sink or bathtub. Soak them for a few hours or until you can bend a stem back and forth a few times without breaking it.

**3** Remove the stems and place them on the towel. Cut off five 15 cm (6 in.) pieces. Choose pieces that are roughly the same width.

**4** Cut eleven pieces of embroidery floss, each 20 cm (8 in.) long. Wet them and squeeze them in the towel so they are damp. Wetting them makes it easier to tie them tightly on the straw.

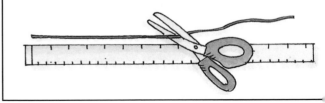

**5** Flatten the center area of each piece of straw between your fingers. It is very important that the stems are lined up side by side with the flattened areas together in the center. When you have them arranged correctly, hold them on each side of the center and ask someone to tie them together with a cut piece of floss. Knot the floss tightly and trim the ends.

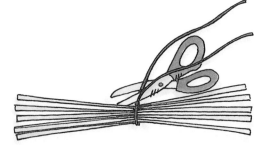

**6** Knot the stems together in pairs about 2.5 cm (1 in.) from the center. Tie them tightly so that the pieces in each pair spread a little apart. Trim all the tying threads.

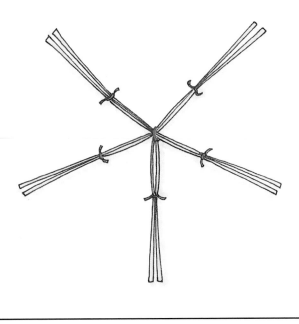

**7** Knot a piece of straw from one pair to a piece of straw from the pair beside it, about 3 cm (1 ¼ in.) from the other row of knots. As you knot your way around the ornament, bend the straws so that the star takes shape. You may find it easier if you hold the stems and have someone else tie the knots for you.

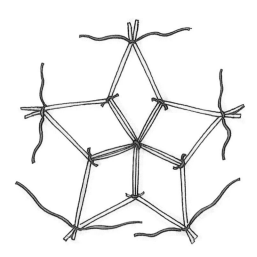

**8** Trim four of the pairs of threads. Tie together the ends of the leftover threads to make a loop so you can hang up your new straw ornament. Dab a bit of nail polish or glue on all the knots. Trim off the straw ends.

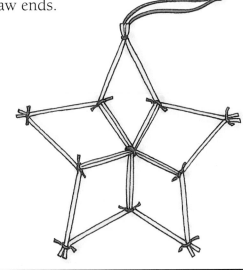

# GERMANY
# Advent calendar

*Children in Germany were the first to count down the days until Christmas. Now this tradition has spread around the world.*
**Frohe Weihnachten!**

## YOU WILL NEED

- a large sheet of newspaper
- a glue stick
- a 55 cm (22 in.) square of corrugated cardboard
- a 55 cm (22 in.) square of fabric, felt or fleece
- masking tape
- 2.5 m (10 ft.) of lace or ribbon
- 24 treats (see step 8 for ideas)
- 24 small paper doilies or tissue paper
- 12 pipe cleaners  • markers (optional)
- a ruler, a pencil, scissors

**1** Fold the newspaper in half and mark a dot 50 cm (20 in.) up along the folded edge. Mark a dot along the bottom edge too, 23 cm (9 in.) from the folded side.

**2** Join the two dots with a wavy pencil line. Make the bottom edge wavy too. Cut out the paper pattern, open it and glue the tree shape onto the cardboard. Cut it out.

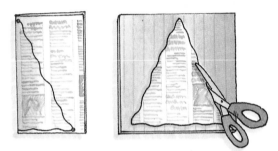

**3** Outline the tree with the glue stick. Place it glue side down onto the wrong side of the fabric. Turn the tree over and smooth the covering over it.

**4** Trim off the extra covering at the edges of the cardboard, or trim it, leaving about 2.5 cm (1 in.) all around, and tape the extra covering to the back. (If you tape it to the back, you may need to make a few cuts in the covering so it fits in the curves of the tree.)

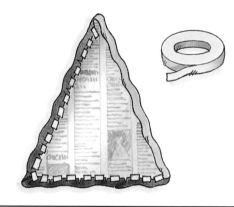

**5** Cut out a cardboard star and cover it with fabric, too. Glue it to the top of the tree. (You may need to use white craft glue.)

**6** Securely tape one end of the lace near the top of the back of the tree. Tightly wrap it around the tree so that you end up with four evenly spaced lines of garland on the front. Tape the lace near the bottom of the back of the tree and trim off any extra.

**7** Tape a loop of ribbon on the back near the top of the tree so you can hang it up.

**8** Gather 24 small treats, such as candies, coins, chocolates, erasers, beads, dice, gum, marbles, jokes on slips of paper, small plastic cars or animals, zipper pulls, marzipan treats, small tree ornaments, inexpensive earrings, pretty stones, trinkets or other small items. Place a treat in the center of each doily and fasten it closed with a half of a pipe cleaner. Prepare each treat the same way. Numbering them is optional.

**9** Shape the ends of the pipe cleaners into hooks and hang the treats on the garland on the Advent calendar tree. Take turns with your family or friends opening one treat each day, starting on December 1st. When all the treats are gone, it will be Christmas Eve!

# ITALY

# Nativity scene

*Centuries ago, Saint Francis of Assisi gathered together people and animals to re-create the first Christmas. The tradition of the nativity scene spread from its beginnings in Italy to homes around the world.*
**Buon Natale!**

**Note:** *If you use fabric to make these figures, apply a little white glue to the cut edges so they do not fray.*

1 Cut out a 12 cm x 22 cm (4½ in. x 8½ in.) rectangle of felt. Fold it in half lengthwise, then widthwise to find the center. Make a small cut at this center point.

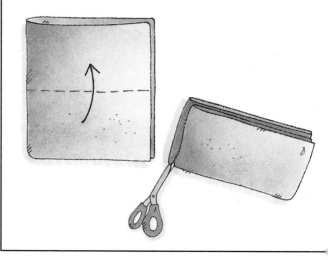

**2** Bend a pipe cleaner in half. Wrap a half pipe cleaner once around the bent pipe cleaner 2 cm (¾ in.) down from the bend. This makes your figure's arms, neck and body.

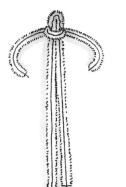

**3** Slip the neck through the hole in the felt rectangle. Bend the pipe-cleaner hands around the edge of the robe to hold it in place.

**4** Spread glue on the neck and put on the wooden bead head.

**5** Bend the arms at the elbows and move them forward. This should bring the robe together in the front. Overlap and glue it. Trim off the pipe-cleaner legs (and the robe if you need to) so that your figure can stand up. For a kneeling pose, bend your figure at the knees.

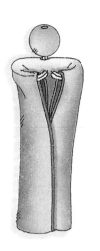

**6** Use the ideas below to make Mary, Joseph, baby Jesus, the kings, a shepherd, an angel, a manger, a stable, a star and sheep. Use paint or markers to make the faces.

### ★ MARY

Glue yarn on Mary's head for hair. Cut a strip of felt for her to wear over her head. Bend her arms to hold baby Jesus.

### ★ JOSEPH

Use markers, paint or yarn to give Joseph hair and a beard.

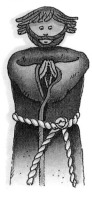

### ★ BABY JESUS

Bend a 5 cm (2 in.) piece of pipe cleaner in half and poke it into a small wooden bead with a bit of glue. Cut a 1 cm x 8 cm (½ in. x 3 in.) strip of felt to glue around the baby's head and tuck under his chin. Twist the strip around the pipe cleaner to hold it in place. Cut a piece of felt to wrap around the baby like a blanket. Glue or stitch it in place.

*Instructions continue on the next page* ☞   33

## ✭ SHEPHERD

Give the shepherd yarn hair, a beard and a pipe-cleaner staff.

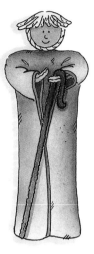

## ✭ ANGEL

Dress the angel in white or light colors. Cut out a large felt heart and glue it on her back to make wings. Decorate her with glitter, ribbon or lace. Make a halo out of a tinsel pipe cleaner and poke it down the hole in the bead head. Glue on yarn hair or tie yarn around the halo and style it.

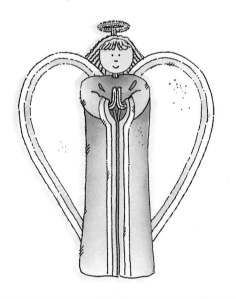

## ✭ KINGS

Dress the kings in colorful robes. Use fancy fabric, or glue special trims onto the sleeves and fronts of the robes. Cut out crowns from shiny greeting cards or ribbon. Glue interesting beads or other trinkets into the kings' hands to represent the gifts they bring for baby Jesus.

## ✭ MANGER

Cut a bathroom-tissue roll in half lengthwise and cut a 6 cm (2¼ in.) piece. Line it with felt. Cut up yellow yarn to look like straw.

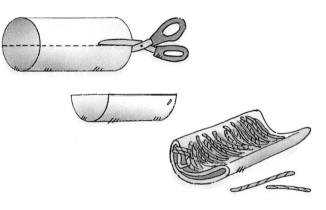

## ✭ STABLE

Cut two simple house shapes about 25 cm (10 in.) tall and 20 cm (8 in.) wide out of cardboard. Cut one in half. Spread glue on one side of each of the three shapes and lay them on squares of felt. Smooth the felt onto the cardboard and trim off any extra. Place the cut house on top of the other one so the felt surfaces are together. To make hinges, cut four short pieces of ribbon. Tape them, two on each side, to the half houses. Now flip the house shapes over and tape the other end of the ribbon onto the back. Open the half houses and set up the stable. Place your nativity figures in and around the stable.

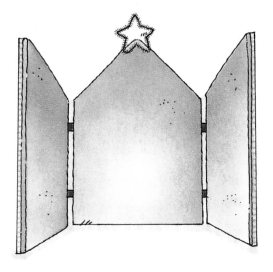

## ✭ STAR

Bend the first 2.5 cm (1 in.) of a tinsel or regular pipe cleaner. Now bend the rest of it into a zigzag pattern using the bent end as a guide. Shape the pipe cleaner into a five-pointed star. Twist the ends around each other and trim off any extra. Hang the star from the top of the stable.

## ✭ SHEEP

**1.** Cut five 75 cm (30 in.) lengths of yarn. Untwist and pull apart the strands of yarn so that you have kinky strands.

**2.** Cut a 15 cm (6 in.) piece of pipe cleaner and bend both ends toward the center, then bend one end down to make the nose. Raise the neck up and push the tail down, as shown.

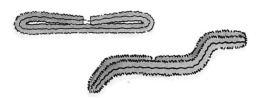

**3.** Cut a 4 cm (1½ in.) piece of pipe cleaner and wrap it around the head to make ears. Cut two 8 cm (3 in.) pieces and wrap them around the body to make four legs.

**4.** Loosely wrap the kinky yarn around the sheep's frame. Leave the ears, nose, legs and tail unwrapped. You don't need to glue the yarn ends — just tuck them under the yarn.

# PHILIPPINES
# Star parol

*Christmas in the Philippines just wouldn't be complete without beautiful star lanterns, called* **parols.**
**Maligayang Pasko!**

## YOU WILL NEED

- a skein of embroidery floss
- 10 pieces of balsa wood, each 0.3 cm (⅛ in.) thick, 0.5 cm (¼ in.) wide and 30 cm (12 in.) long (page 5)
- thick white glue
- 5 short pieces of balsa wood, each 4 cm (1½ in.) long
- a 40 cm (16 in.) piece of ribbon or cord
- 2 or more sheets of different-colored tissue paper
- a ruler, scissors

1 Cut twenty 30 cm (12 in.) pieces of embroidery floss.

2 Make a star shape out of five long balsa pieces. Fasten two pieces together at one of the points of the star by wrapping a piece of floss around the point four or five times and tightly knotting the ends. Fasten the other four points of the star in this same way. **Do not trim off the floss ends.**

3 Make another star the same way, but on the second star trim off the threads and dab glue on the knots.

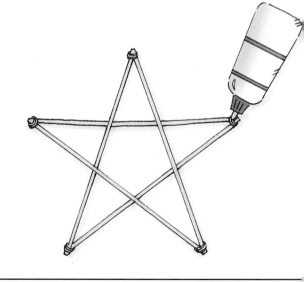

4 Adjust the second, trimmed star until you are happy with its shape. Keep this shape by tying the balsa pieces together where they cross on the inside area of the star. Trim all the threads and dab glue on the knots.

5 Place the tied and trimmed star on top of the other star. Use the embroidery floss ends at each point to fasten the two stars together. Trim the ends and dab glue on the knots.

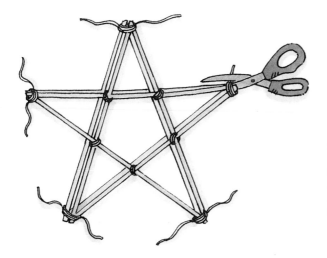

6 Apply glue to each end of one of the short pieces of balsa. Very carefully, separate the two stars and place the piece of balsa between them. (You may find this step easier if someone holds the stars apart for you.) Glue the other four pieces in place, too.

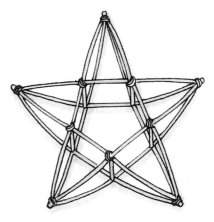

7 Tie the ribbon on one point of the star. You will need to keep it out of the way when you glue on the tissue.

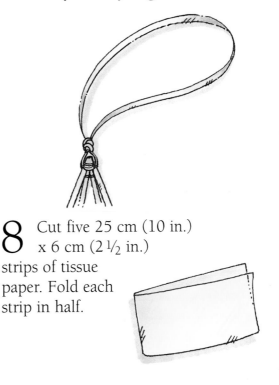

8 Cut five 25 cm (10 in.) x 6 cm (2 ½ in.) strips of tissue paper. Fold each strip in half.

*Instructions continue on the next page* ☞

**9** Gently hold one of the star points between your knees. Apply glue to the four side edges of the star frame facing you.

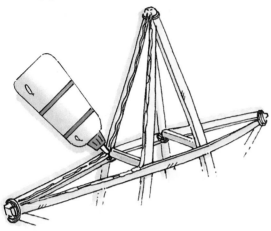

**10** Smooth a strip of tissue onto the glued areas. Wrap the extra tissue around the points and the sides of the frame. Make small cuts at the corners to keep the tissue smooth. Trim off all the tissue not glued down. Fill in the other sides of the star with the other strips of tissue paper and trim off any extra.

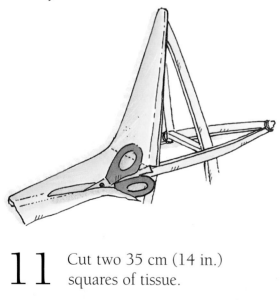

**11** Cut two 35 cm (14 in.) squares of tissue.

**12** Spread glue along the front of the star frame. Place one of the tissue squares over it. Pull the tissue gently until it is smooth. Trim the tissue close to the edges of the star, being very careful to not poke the tissue on the sides of the frame. Again, cut the corners and glue any extra tissue over the edges.

**13** Cover the other side of the star with tissue, too. If you break through the tissue while you are covering the star, either glue on a tissue-paper patch or tear off the tissue in that area and re-cover it.

**14** Make tassels by cutting many tissue-paper strips, each about 20 cm (8 in.) long and 5 cm (2 in.) wide. (Cut strips quickly by folding the tissue paper and cutting many layers at a time.) Place six strips in a pile. Twist them together in the center then fold the bundle in half. Make lots of cuts in the bundle so that it looks like a tassel.

**16** Trim the other tie end a little and glue it to one of the two lower points of the star. Make at least one more tassel or enough for four points of the star.

**15** Take another strip and twist it until it is narrow, but strong. Use it to tie the tassel about 1 cm (½ in.) down from the top. Knot the strip and let one end hang down with the tassel.

**17** Hang up your parol in a window or from the ceiling, away from a candle or hot lightbulb.

# Christmas sharing

*All around the world, Christmas is a time when people are generous to those in need. Here are some crafty ideas to get you thinking of ways in which you can show you care at Christmas. Drop off your donation at a local church, shelter or charity.*

## ✶ Storytime basket

Get a wicker basket, or paint a cardboard fruit basket with acrylic craft paint and decorate it with drawings or stickers. Line the basket with napkins or tissue paper and put in hot chocolate mix, mugs, cookies and a few good children's books.

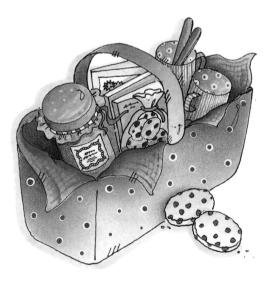

## ✶ Craft-time box

Decorate a box with a flip-top lid, or get a small plastic bin and fill it with craft supplies. Markers, crayons, construction paper, pipe cleaners, scissors, glue, stickers, beads, yarn, felt, pom-poms and any of your other favorite craft materials are all perfect to inspire hours of fun.

## ✶ Bags of joy

Make the Sinterklaas sack (page 12) or Festive pillowcase (page 22) and put in special new toys, warm clothing or groceries.

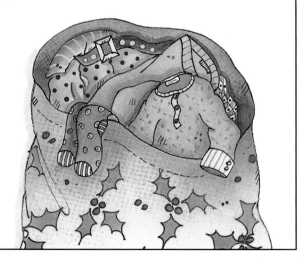